Dear Kids
of Alcoholics

Lindsey Hall & Leigh Cohn
Illustrations by
Rosemary E. Lingenfelter

Gürze Books

Dear Kids of Alcoholics

©1988 by Lindsey Hall and Leigh Cohn
Illustrations ©1988 by Rosemary E. Lingenfelter

A special thank you to Ross Barber

Gürze Books
P.O. Box 2238
Carlsbad, CA 92008
(619) 434-7533

Library of Congress Cataloging-in-Publication Data

Hall, Lindsey, 1949-
    Dear kids of alcoholics / by Lindsey Hall & Leigh Cohn
Illustrated by Rosemary E. Lingenfelter
    p. cm.
Summary: A young boy imparts facts about alcoholism by discussing his father's sensitivity to alcohol, destructive behavior, and recovery process.
    1. Alcoholism--Juvenile literature. 2. Children of alcoholics--Juvenile literature. [1. Alcoholism. 2. Alcoholics--Family relationships.] I. Cohn, Leigh. II. Lingenfelter, Rosemary E., ill. III. Title.
    HV5066.H35   1988   88-24735
    362.2'92--dc19   CIP   AC

ISBN 0-936077-18-2 (pbk.) : $6.95

10 9 8 7 6 5 4 3 2

Table of Contents

"I hope by writing my story, I can help. . ."

INTRODUCTION

I'm Jason

I love my Dad, but I used to think he hated me, my Mom, and my teen-aged sister, Jennifer. Our home was not a fun place to live.

Dad was usually mad, he lied a lot, and we could never trust him. I was afraid of him, and I worried that bad things would happen to me and my family. Lots of times, Dad yelled at me when I didn't think I was doing anything wrong.

When he came home from work, the first thing he always did was have a drink. Sometimes, he kept drinking all night. On weekends, he kept a can of beer within reach at all times. He was a drinker since before I was born, so I didn't think anything of it. I had no way of knowing that it was his drinking that made him get mad, forgetful, or sick.

I didn't understand that most of our family's problems were because Dad drank too much **alcohol**, which is a chemical in beer, wine, and other liquor. Someone who drinks so much that they cannot stop themselves is called an **alcoholic.**

Dad is now a **recovering alcoholic**. He says he had to quit drinking because he could not drink just a little and stop. If he had even one sip of wine, he wanted more and more.

Giving up alcohol has been hard for Dad, but important for our whole family. We've all changed for the better since he stopped drinking. We never used to talk about our feelings with anyone. In fact, we acted like we didn't even have feelings. Talking to each other has helped us to find out and show that we love and care about each other.

When I finally stopped hiding the truth about Dad, I found that I did not always have to be afraid, guilty, and worried. It was a great relief for me to tell my school counselor about my problems at home, and I now see that there were other people who would have listened to me, like a good adult friend or close relative.

I've learned a lot about alcohol and people who drink too much. I think kids feel hurt because **alcoholism** is in their homes. I hope by writing my story, I can help them understand about being children of alcoholics, and then maybe they'll feel better about themselves, too.

I love my Dad, and now I know that he loves me.

CHAPTER 1

The Invisible Boy

I suppose most people thought we were a pretty normal family. I thought we were a pretty normal family, too—whatever that meant.

I figured most parents fought; and, all fathers yelled at their kids, worked, and were too busy to do things like help with homework, go places, or just be there to talk. I believed that all moms took care of everyone's problems, had a million things to do, talked on the phone a lot, and sometimes sat alone crying.

Older sisters, like Jennifer, had to be a mistake of nature for all the trouble they caused. I didn't know much about brothers. I mean, I'm a brother, but you'd have to ask Jennie to know what brothers are really like. Besides, she thinks I'm invisible, anyway.

As a matter of fact, lots of times when Dad was still drinking, I felt like I *was* invisible and often wished that I were. It seemed like everyone in the house was weird except me.

I wondered if I was adopted or maybe got switched with another baby in the hospital when I was born. Sometimes I imagined what it would be like to have parents who really loved me and went on family picnics or to ball games. One day, this idea got so big in my mind that whenever the phone rang, I believed it was my real parents calling to say that they discovered the foul up. They were coming over to get me and would be dropping off Mom and Dad's real son, who was a total jerk like them.

"I felt like I was invisible. . ."

For all the trouble alcohol caused my family, I might not be here if Dad wasn't drinking the night he met Mom. I heard him tell the story lots of times. They were at a party, and he was looking at her from across the room. His friend said, "Tom, why don't you introduce yourself to her."

"No, she might think I'm a jerk," Dad said, because he was too shy.

After he had drunk a couple of beers, Dad started to feel less shy from the alcohol. He was telling jokes to his friends, and when they laughed, he looked at Mom to see if she noticed him. After drinking a third beer, the alcohol made him have even more courage, and he introduced himself to her.

Of course, they liked each other and went on dates and eventually got married. The way Dad tells it, though, he never would have talked to her in the first place if he wasn't a little drunk.

Before he quit drinking, Dad wasn't around much, and when he was home, he'd be drunk or passed out on the sofa. If I wanted to turn on the television or stereo, Mom would yell at me not to wake him. I learned to be quiet and keep out of the way, which just made me feel lonely and sad. It made me think there was something wrong with me.

Dad got drunk so much that he started having **blackouts**. He would completely forget things he did and said.

One time I brought a paper home from school about a field trip. I gave it to him and said, "Dad, my class is going to a museum this week and you have to read and sign this paper."

"I'll look at it in the kitchen," he said. "Just leave me alone for a few minutes."

When I went into the kitchen to get it from him, he was drinking a beer.

"Did you sign that permission sheet for me?" I asked.

"What are you talking about?" he replied.

"I gave you a paper from my teacher. You said you'd read it in the kitchen."

"Did you get in trouble in school?" he accused.

"No, the paper was about going on a field trip, and I had to get your signature."

"I don't have time for that now," he said, taking another beer from the refrigerator. "Tell your mother to take care of it."

"But you took the paper from me," I replied, worried I wouldn't be allowed to go.

"I don't have your paper," he said. "You have to keep better track of your things, Jason," he snapped, pointing his finger at me. I felt my face get red and my eyes fill with tears. I held them back, afraid that if I cried he would get *really* mad at me.

Then Dad walked out of the room. I thought it was my fault for not getting the paper signed, and I felt guilty for getting him upset. I didn't know what to do.

Now I realize it was the alcohol that made him act that way. It wasn't my fault at all.

I found the paper on the kitchen counter by the phone. He had signed it, but completely forgot. He had had a **blackout.**

"I found the paper on the kitchen counter by the phone."

Other kids at school had a lot of friends, but I pretty much stayed to myself. I was afraid to get close to anyone. If I did, they might come over to my house and see what a mess my life really was. Who wants to have someone think you're kind of special and then see you at home being treated like you don't exist? What if they saw my parents fighting and Dad drunk? Maybe he'd yell at my friend or even hit him. Instead, my only friendships were with the imaginary characters in books, and I spent a lot of my time reading alone.

So there you have it. I was invisible and had invisible friends.

I've learned that it's common for families of alcoholics to keep **secrets** about what goes on at home. It was an unspoken rule in our family not to tell other people about Dad's drinking or our other problems. No one ever said to me, "Jason, be sure you never tell anyone that Dad drinks a lot," or anything like that. None of us ever talked about his drinking.

We acted like if we didn't talk about our problems, then maybe they didn't really exist. **Denial** is common in families of alcoholism. That means not admitting that anything is wrong.

In fact, when we were supposed to write stories about ourselves for school, I lied and pretended that my family was great. Of course it wasn't, but I was too embarrassed to tell the truth. When I finally talked to my school counselor about how bad it was at home, it actually was a great relief to be honest.

Look, I want to be seen now. Since Dad started to get **sober**, not drinking any more, all of our lives changed for the better. But, more on that later.

J-e-n-n-i-f-e-r Spells Trouble!

While I sometimes imagined that I was adopted, I believed that my sister Jennifer was an alien from outer space. I often wished she'd get sent back there!

Jennie usually stayed away from the house, but when she did show up at home, she made things worse. She was always in trouble.

Maybe I wasn't a straight-A student, but a gorilla could have gotten better grades than Jennie. I thought she was pretty smart, but I guess she just never tried to do well. She must have made an effort to do poorly, because as Dad's drinking got worse, so did her grades and behavior at school. Getting in trouble was her way to get attention.

The thing was, the more she messed up, the angrier Mom and Dad got, and the worse they treated her. You'd think she'd get the hint after being punished, yelled at, and worse; but, Jennie just kept getting in more and more trouble.

The time <u>she</u> came home drunk was really a bad scene. Jennie said she was going to the mall and a movie with some other girls. I don't know if that's how the evening started out or not, but she got driven home close to midnight by some guy I'd never seen before. I know because I saw them from my bedroom window. They were kissing and he had his hands all over her.

When she walked in the door, Mom was there waiting. I spied on them from the stairs.

"Why are you so late?" Mom asked.

"After the movie, we went over to a party for a little while, and then Sara drove me home."

I couldn't believe it. Jennie just lied as if Mom couldn't have looked out the window like I had and seen that it wasn't Sara's car.

"You said you would be home right after the movie," Mom said. I guess she missed seeing the car.

"Well, I didn't know we'd be going to a party, so how could I know I wouldn't be home right after the movie."

"You should have called," Mom said. "I stayed up worrying because you didn't come home. I was afraid something might have happened to you. You made me *crazy* worrying!"

If it were me, I would have just agreed with Mom and apologized. That would have ended the conversation, but not Jennie. No, she looked for trouble.

"I don't even know if they had a phone there," she said. "Besides, I don't have to tell you everything I do. I'm in high school. I'm not a baby. I can do whatever I want." She turned her back and started to walk out of the room.

Mom got mad. "If you think this is over, you're quite wrong." She grabbed Jennie's arm, "You smell like wine! Have you been drinking?"

"No, I just had a little punch at the party," Jennie replied, but then she started giggling.

"You're drunk!" Mom exclaimed.

"Oh, give me a break," she laughed in a kind of nasty way, throwing her hands in the air.

"You're not allowed to drink," Mom said. "Who got the wine for you?"

"Oh please," Jennie sneered, raising her voice, "leave me alone. All the kids drink. So I had a glass of wine at a party, big deal."

"Were there adults there?"

"Mom, I'm not a baby. It was a college party. It wasn't for little kids." she said in a loud voice. "Besides, there's nothing wrong with having a little wine. If you can do it, so can I. So get off my case!"

That was saying the wrong thing at the wrong time, because Dad walked in, and he looked furious.

Sometimes I liked it when Jennie got in trouble, but when I saw the angry expression on Dad's face, I was worried for her. I wished I could make everything better for them, but there was nothing I could do but remain unseen.

"What's all the ruckus about? You woke me up."

"It's nothing," Mom said, not wanting to get Dad upset. We were all afraid of getting Dad angry. Usually when there was a problem, Mom took care of it; but this time Dad wasn't going back to bed.

"Did she just get home?" he demanded.

Mom told him that Jennie came home late, and it wasn't long before Dad heard the whole story. First, he yelled at Mom, saying that everything was her fault. Then, Jennie defended Mom, saying that she chose to go to the party, not Mom. That led Dad to his usual routine of getting about a foot away from Jennie, pointing his finger in her face, and calling her all kinds of words that I'm not allowed to say.

"You're grounded for a month," Dad told her, but I doubted he'd even remember the punishment the next morning. "If I ever catch you drinking again, you'll really be sorry."

"I'll do what I want," she answered in a low voice.

It was definitely the wrong thing to say! Dad reached back and slapped her so hard on the cheek that she fell back on to the couch. Both Jennie and Mom started crying, and Dad stormed out muttering, "Don't you ever talk back to me again."

He went in another room to pour himself a drink. Whatever the problem, the solution for Dad was to take a drink.

I can't remember if Dad ever hit Jennie before that night, but that was not the last time he hit her or Mom, either. When Dad was drinking, I made sure to stay out of trouble or out of sight, because I was afraid that he might hit me, too.

Fortunately, he never did, though he did lock me in a closet once as punishment. It seemed unfair that I would have to sit in a dark closet just because I forgot to give him a phone message. Besides, the guy on the phone said he'd call back later anyway, and he did.

I was very scared. I knew Dad sometimes had blackouts and forgot things. What if he forgot about me and I had to stay in the closet forever? I remembered he was cooking something on the stove. What if he left it there and it caught fire? The whole house might burn down, and I would be killed. He might leave the house and crash the car again. No one would find me. He did remember me that time though, and about an hour later, he let me out for dinner.

I'm ashamed to say it, but there were lots of times I wished he would die, because then I would not have to be so afraid anymore. Life would be peaceful and simple. Mom wouldn't have to worry so much either, and she could give me more love. Part of me really thought we would be better off if he was dead, and another part of me felt horrible for feeling that way.

When you live with an alcoholic, you never know what's going to happen. You don't like your family and you don't feel good about yourself. I'm here to tell you, though, that there is hope for happiness and love if the alcoholic in your family quits drinking.

CHAPTER 2

Nothing to Brag About

For most of my life, Dad bragged that he could "drink everyone under the table," which meant he could drink more than they could without getting sick. For fun, Dad and his friends drank until some of the guys would start to vomit or faint. Dad used to keep drinking longer than any of them. I don't know why they thought it was fun.

Most of his buddies got **hangovers**, which means they felt really sick the next morning after being drunk. Dad says he never had a hangover. He was proud of that.

When people used to tell Dad he shouldn't drink so much, he used to say that it was okay because he mainly drank beer, which wasn't as bad as liquor.

I didn't understand. I knew that kids weren't allowed to drink beer, wine, or liquors like vodka or Scotch. I thought drinks were all alike, because they all had alcohol in them. So when Dad used to say it was okay to drink beer, I was confused.

I found out that some kinds of drinks have more alcohol in them than others. The <u>alcohol is the same drug in each</u>, but the amount is different.

About 1 1/2 ounces of liquor (a shot glass full, or as much as is put into a cocktail), has as much alcohol in it as 5 ounces of wine (about half of a wine glass) or 12 ounces of beer (one regular sized can).

A bottle of whiskey has about the same amount as a little more than three bottles of wine or three six-packs (eighteen cans) of beer.

Whether someone drinks three or four cocktails or a few beers, they still are getting enough alcohol to get drunk.

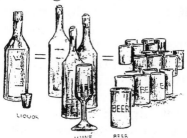

"Alcohol is the same drug in many kinds of drinks."

Mom once told me about a time quite a few years ago when she and Dad went out to dinner with friends of theirs, the Macks. Before they picked up the Macks, Dad wanted a drink to relax. He had a Scotch on the rocks—about two ounces of very strong alcohol and ice. I feel dizzy even smelling a glass of Scotch!

At the restaurant, they each had a drink at the bar while waiting for their table, and Dad had another one when they sat down. Most social drinkers would have felt pretty "light-headed" after that much to drink, but not an alcoholic.

During dinner they shared three bottles of wine, and Mom said that Dad drank as much as the rest of them put together. Dad and Mr. Mack also had "after dinner liqueurs," sugary, strong alcoholic drinks. She didn't have one because she was feeling kind of dizzy from the wine.

Dad said they were all having such a good time, he offered to buy another round of drinks. No one else wanted one, but he had another Scotch on the rocks anyway.

Even though he drank much more than the others, he was not as drunk as everyone else. They all knew that Dad could "hold his liquor," which meant he could drink a lot without getting drunk. He convinced them that he was fine, so they let him drive home.

On the way home, Dad crashed the car into a telephone pole. He said a cat ran across the road and he was trying to miss hitting it, but Mom told me that he was too drunk to see straight.

The car needed to be towed away, and Mrs. Mack had to go to the hospital. She wore a brace on her neck for almost a whole year. Mr. Mack was mad at Dad, and Dad kept blaming the cat. Dad never admitted that he was too drunk to drive.

My parents aren't friends with the Macks anymore.

Alcohol is a Drug

Alcohol changes how well the brain works. The brain is the main part of the **central nervous system**, which controls body movements, the senses, thoughts, emotions, and even dreams.

When anyone drinks beer, wine, or other alcoholic beverages, alcohol enters their body. It mixes with their blood. Then it gets into the muscle tissue and all of the organs, like the brain, heart, liver, and kidneys.

When alcohol starts to affect the brain, it is a **stimulant**. That's a drug that increases energy levels in the central nervous system. If someone has a drink, at first they may have more energy, feel more relaxed, and have more confidence in themselves. They may feel better about themselves, and often will say or do things that they might usually be too afraid to do—like when Dad "drank up the courage" to talk to Mom for the first time.

Although alcohol starts out as a stimulant, it becomes a **depressant**. That is a drug that lowers the energy of the central nervous system. As people drink more, their thinking and actions get slower. That's what it means to be **drunk**. For a little while it feels good to be drunk, but later the person feels pretty sick.

Even though he felt really good when he got behind the wheel, Dad was drunk! That's why he wrecked the car.

Memories

I don't want you to think my family life was always lousy. It wasn't. There were times that Dad was cheerful and a pretty nice guy to be around. Usually Mom was home, asked me about school, fixed me snacks, and gave me hugs when I needed them. Even Jennie had her decent moments, like when she let me do my homework in her room and we listened to the radio together.

I remember going out for dinner to fancy restaurants, where Mom and Dad had cocktails and Jennie and I drank fancy sodas which looked like cocktails but didn't have any alcohol in them. Those were happy days. It was cool to bite the cherry off of the long, plastic toothpick (it was shaped like a sword!) and to sip the sweet, red soda from skinny straws like Mom had in her cocktail. Jennie always said it looked "so glamorous" to sip her drink, and it did. But believe me, I now understand that there is nothing glamorous about someone who drinks too much.

One time I drank bourbon. I had seen Jennie drink it with one of her friends when Mom and Dad weren't home. I thought I would see for myself what it was like. I had wanted to try drinking alcohol for a long time, to be more like an adult.

That afternoon, I was alone watching an old western movie on television. It was a pretty good film, with this one good guy who helped people by shooting bad guys. In one scene, he walked into a saloon and asked the bartender for whiskey. As the bartender cleaned off a glass and put it on the bar, a young punk kicked open the swinging doors of the saloon and pulled his gun. He was going to let the good guy have it in the back! In one motion, the hero crouched, turned, shot the pistol out of the punk's hand, blasted the hat off his head, and then calmly stood up, faced the bar again, and gulped down the whiskey in one swallow.

I put on a toy holster and cowboy hat and then went to the liquor cabinet and wiped off a shot glass, one of those small glasses that holds about an ounce. I poured it about halfway full with bourbon and set the glass on the counter. I pretended that I was the guy in the movie, turned away and shot an imaginary bad guy. Then I gulped down the bourbon.

It tasted horrible! My mouth and throat felt like they were on fire and my eyes started to water. I could feel it burning its way all the way to my stomach. I started coughing and couldn't catch my breath. I thought I would die!

I can't believe my Dad could actually drink a whole bottle of that stuff without dropping dead. From what I've learned about alcohol, he really was slowly killing himself.

"I pretended that I was the guy in the movie."

CHAPTER 3

Excuses

As Dad's drinking problem got more and more out of control, Mom changed in certain ways, too. Someone who is affected by an alcoholic and changes their own behavior—like Mom did—is called a **codependent**. A codependent will try to take care of everyone else's problems. They worry a lot, feel guilty and embarrassed about the alcoholic's drinking, keep busy, and even though they are very angry, codependents may not show their anger.

Mom was like that when Dad was still drinking. She was always telling me and Jennie what to do, even little things. Like if Jennie picked out a red shirt to wear, Mom would complain and say that she should wear a blue shirt. If Jennie said she was going to take a bus somewhere, Mom would drive her instead, acting like it was a really big inconvenience and all. She made us feel like we could never do the right thing without her help.

She tried to make Dad feel that way, too. That's pretty common for codependents. I think she thought that if she took care of everything, Dad would eventually get better, and <u>then</u> we could be a happy family.

I'd be a millionaire if I had a dollar for every time Mom told Dad he shouldn't drink so much. She'd say things like, "Tom, if you come home late again because you went out drinking, you'll have to get your own dinner." But, every time it happened, Mom saved dinner for him, served it to him, and then bugged him all through the meal, complaining about how annoyed she was.

Dad's usual response was to tell her to shut up and grab a beer from the refrigerator to "calm" himself. Then he blamed her, saying something like, "It's your fault that I drink. Listen to yourself. The way you go on and on all the time, no wonder I need to drink. Who would want to live with you and stay sober?"

She made threats and then didn't follow through on them. So he just went on treating her in a pretty lousy way, and she just went on as if everything was just fine.

Mom's Night Out

One time Mom made plans to meet some of her friends for dinner. She was really looking forward to it, because she didn't get to go out with her friends very often. She spent as much time getting dressed and putting on makeup as Jennie does before going out on a date. Dad had promised to be home early enough for her to meet her friends by six o'clock.

Around 5:30 he called to say he might be a few minutes late, because he was at a bar with a business client. He came home drunk almost three hours later, though, and Mom got really upset.

"Susan, I'm sorry," he apologized. "This guy is an important client, and I couldn't just walk away."

"But you promised to be home, Tom" she said.

"I know, and I thought I would be. How should I know the guy would want to keep talking all night. What could I do?"

Dad grabbed a beer from the refrigerator.

"Didn't you tell him you had to go? What about Jason? He was looking forward to going out to dinner with you." Mom asked, making it seem like I was the one—not her—who was so disappointed.

"What did you expect me to say? 'I have to go because my kid wants to get a hamburger.' That would have made me look like a real idiot."

I was pretty disappointed, but I guess I was used to him letting me down. Hearing him say that really made me feel worthless, like he didn't care about me at all.

"No, you would have seemed like a father who cares about his son."

"Right," Dad said with disbelief, "He's a single guy. He wouldn't understand that, and I would have been insulting him. He wanted to have a few drinks, so I had to stay with him. It's my job."

"But what about us? You completely ruined my night and Jason's, too. We're your family. Doesn't that matter."

"How can you be so selfish," Dad answered. "What do you think I work eight hours a day for? Fun? Look, Susan, I work hard for you and the kids. Period. I don't need your telling me that I don't care about you , because I do care."

"I know you do," she softened. "It's just that I was really looking forward to tonight, and now I missed the whole party."

"Well, don't blame me," he said, "I came home as soon as I could. You can still go and get there for the end of it."

"Well,
don't blame me,"
he said.

Alcoholics lie a lot. In the first place, Dad's client probably left hours before he did, or maybe there never was any client. Maybe Dad just made up that excuse to get Mom off his back. Also, as soon as she started saying he was wrong, he turned the whole conversation around to make it seem like it was her fault for not appreciating his hard work. They never even mentioned that he had been drinking too much. They both pretended that alcohol had nothing to do with it.

Then, Mom refused to go to the restaurant. She said she'd be embarrassed to get there so late. I suppose she could have gone, but I think she preferred staying home and being miserable. That way she could remind him of how bad she felt for days to come.

There were times like that when I hated being in my family.

Who is Alcoholic?

I was confused.

Beer and wine are advertised on television commercials all of the time. It looks like fun to drink. But there was nothing fun about my Dad when he'd come home drunk after "entertaining" clients or drinking with friends. He would spend whole weekends drinking beer and getting more and more angry with each can.

Even after Dad quit drinking, Mom sometimes still had a glass of wine when she wanted one. Why was it all right for her to drink but he couldn't?

Most adults drink alcohol. Most are **social drinkers**. They can enjoy drinking once in a while without having to keep drinking. That's called **drinking in moderation**.

People, like Dad, who are alcoholics, drink too much and too often. About <u>one out of every ten</u> people who drink cannot stop themselves. Unlike social drinkers, once an alcoholic starts drinking, they usually keep drinking for as long as they are awake and there is anything left to drink. Many alcoholics get drunk every day. Others go on "binges" and just drink heavily for a few days in a row.

Experts are not sure why some people become alcoholics and others don't. They say that the kind of home and culture that people come from have a lot to do with it.

Most experts also think that some people may be more likely to become alcoholics because of **heredity**, which means that they were born with certain kinds of characteristics inherited from one or both of their parents. In the same way that someone may have their mother's hair color or grandfather's height, they may also have difficulty drinking alcohol, like one of their parents or grandparents.

I sometimes worry that I will become an alcoholic like my Dad. Maybe I've inherited the same characteristics from him that made him become alcoholic. I've obviously been in a home where drinking takes place. My only hope is that I know enough to not drink too much— ever.

CHAPTER 4

Dad's Boss Visits

Around dinner time one Friday night, Dad's boss, Mr. Hardy, came to the door.

"Hello, Jason," he said. "Is your father home?"

"No, he's not home yet," I answered.

Mom heard him and came to the doorway.

"Hello, Susan," he said, "Tom's not home yet?"

"No, he's running a little late tonight. He had to make a stop on his way home from work."

"I see. May I come in?" Mr. Hardy asked.

I could see Mom hesitate before answering. We didn't like to have people come over, because they might ask questions. They might find out about our secrets. She did invite him in, though, and I listened as they spoke in serious voices.

"So how is everything?" he asked. "I haven't seen you for a while."

"Oh, just fine," she said in a matter-of-fact way, like people usually answer that question.

"That's nice," he said, but I was wondering why he came. "Does Tom get home this late most nights?"

"Oh no, hardly ever," she lied. Actually, Dad came home late almost every night, but she wasn't about to tell Mr. Hardy that. "Tonight, he had a lot to do. In fact, he probably won't be home for a couple of hours," she said, hoping that Mr. Hardy would not wait around and maybe catch Dad as he stumbled home smelling of booze.

"Well, I'm kind of glad that he's not here. That will give us a chance to talk if you have a few minutes."

"Um, the kids and I were about to sit down to dinner. . ." She wanted to get rid of him.

"This shouldn't take too long, Susan, but it's important. I have to talk to you about Tom," Mr. Hardy insisted. Since he was Dad's boss, Mom couldn't refuse. She sent me upstairs, but I stopped halfway to listen.

"Is he having trouble at work?"

"Yes, I'm afraid he is. I like Tom. He's been a good employee for several years, and that's why I wanted to talk to you before I took any other kind of action."

"What do you mean, Mr. Hardy?" she asked, sounding worried.

"Tom has been coming in late quite often lately, and in fact he didn't even show up at work today," Mr. Hardy said.

"Oh no!"

"A number of his clients have complained that he has been irresponsible, and I think he may have a drinking problem."

"No, I don't think so. Everyone knows that Tom can hold his liquor," Mom said, defending Dad.

"I'm not so sure," Mr. Hardy replied. "He goes out for long lunches and either returns a little 'high' or sometimes doesn't come back at all. His work habits have gotten poor. He is not being responsible with his clients. He comes in late and is absent from work fairly often. I think alcohol has gotten the best of him."

Mom continued to deny that Dad had a problem even though she was ashamed of his drinking. It was as if his failures were her own. She felt that she should have been able to make him stop drinking.

Mr. Hardy interrupted her thoughts, "Susan, yesterday I accidentally found him drinking vodka straight out of a bottle in the men's room. He quickly hid the bottle in the trash and thought I didn't see him. Maybe he knew I did see him. Maybe that's why he didn't come in today. That's why I came over here tonight. I wanted to talk to Tom, but I'm actually glad to talk to you first."

"He's been under a lot of pressure," Mom said, still looking for excuses.

"I know that," Mr. Hardy kindly replied, "but he's putting me under pressure, too. I'm not going to be able to cover for him much longer. If Tom can't control his drinking, he'll have to find another job."

"If Tom can't control his drinking, he'll have to find another job."

Mom started to quietly cry.

"Susan, this is not the first time I've known an alcoholic. It's a disease, you know, and it can be treated. Tom needs help. I've always liked him and have had high hopes for him. I believe he can still be an important part of our company, but he has to stop drinking."

"He can stop. I know he can," Mom said.

"Yes, he can," Mr. Hardy agreed. "But Tom needs help. The company insurance program will pay for most of the expenses if he needs treatment, but if he doesn't get help, I'm afraid I'll have to fire him."

"I talk to him about it," Mom said. "I know he'll straighten up."

"I hope so," Mr. Hardy nodded. "I honestly hope so."

After Mr. Hardy left, Mom went into the kitchen to cry. I followed her in there, because I wanted to help. I put my arm around her shoulder, and tried to be of comfort.

Dad Returns

I was sound asleep when my parents' shouting woke me up. This happened often. I rarely got a full night's sleep when Dad was drinking. That night, Mom must have stayed up waiting for him to get home after Mr. Hardy's visit. Dad said he went out with some friends after work, but Mom did not defend him, like she did to Mr. Hardy.

"After work?" she yelled, "You never went to work! Your boss came by the house. He told me that you weren't at work today."

"Hardy came here? Why would he come here? What did you tell him?"

"He came because he's worried about your drinking," Mom replied.

"That's none of his business," Dad said. "Besides, he drinks. He should worry about himself, not me."

"It is his business, Tom, and he's only trying to help."

"I don't need his help," Dad answered.

"Mr. Hardy said you've been drinking at work, that he caught you drinking in the bathroom."

"Who does he think he is, spying on me. For two cents, I'd tell him to take his job and find someone else. "

"Tom, he said you could lose your job."

"He knows I'm too important to the company to fire me. I don't need that lousy job anyway. Someday, I'm going to have my own company and I'll steal away every one of Hardy's customers."

I'd heard Dad talk like that other times. He had grandiose plans, like many alcoholics have. The alcohol makes them think that they will be able to do great things with their lives.

"How are you going to start your own business?" Mom asked. "That would take a lot of money, and we aren't even paying all of our bills now. I'm two months late paying the bank for our house mortgage, we owe money on all of our credit cards, and the phone company would have turned off the telephone if I didn't drive to their offices with the check a few days ago. I'm embarrassed to be seen by our paper boy when he delivers the evening newspaper, because I haven't paid him for three months."

Mom started to cry, and I could hear Dad walking back and forth around the living room.

"I make good money, why isn't there enough?" Dad asked.

"I don't know, Tom," Mom said. "Maybe it costs more to live now than it used to. It's not fair. You always have cash to go out drinking, but I barely have enough to feed the kids decent meals."

"Don't blame me. I don't spend that much drinking."

"Maybe you do," Mom said. "I looked at some of the charge card bills, and you spend $30 or $40 each time you go out. Add beer and Scotch that you drink at home, and I figured that you spend as much on booze as we're supposed to pay for our monthly house mortgage." Mom started crying harder. "Plus, there's all those days you miss work because you're too sick to get out of bed. Tom, your drinking could make us lose our house. You could lose your job. What would happen to us? I don't want to lose everything!"

"We won't," he tried to comfort her. "Susan, it will all be okay, really."

"Please, stop drinking. I can't take it any more. I'm so afraid. Please stop!"

"I will," he promised. "I've been so stupid. I love you too much to keep hurting you this way. I'll quit tomorrow, I will."

I didn't realize that our family was in such trouble. I knew Dad's drinking made him mad and forgetful, but I didn't know it could make him lose his job or make us have to move. I pictured us losing our house and living in a cardboard box somewhere like the homeless people I've heard about so many times. I started to cry, too.

"I pictured us losing our house and living in a cardboard box. . ."

I walked into Jennie's room. I did not want to be alone, and even though she might yell at me, I hoped that she might let me just sit with her for a while. Jennie was awake and had heard it all. She sat on the side of her bed and held out her arms. I sat next to her and cried while she held me. We needed each other and had nowhere else to turn.

CHAPTER 5

On the Wagon

On Saturday, Dad was like a changed man. He kept busy all day, doing yard work, helping Mom clean the house, washing the car. He acted cheerful, and I heard him brag to one of our neighbors that he was **on the wagon**, which meant he wasn't drinking anymore.

I helped, too. I wanted him to appreciate me, to say that I was doing a good job, that he liked having me help. I hoped he would notice me, and he did a little, but mostly he seemed lost in his thoughts and stayed busy.

It was a hot day, and typically he would have had ten or twelve beers on a Saturday at home. Instead, he drank glass after glass of ice water for his thirst.

That night, we watched a television movie, except for Jennie who went to some party. Sitting in front of the tube together, I had the idea that we really were a normal, happy family, and everything would be okay. Dad acted nicer than he had for months, but he looked kind of sick.

I heard him vomiting in the night, and he spent most of Sunday in bed. He had a high fever part of the time and was chilled a lot. Mom said he had a bad case of the flu, but he was actually feeling sick from not drinking.

By Monday morning, he was feeling slightly better, and he insisted on going to work. He and Mom talked on the phone several times during the day, and he promised that he was staying "dry"—not drinking alcohol. He came home right after work, didn't feel good enough to eat dinner, and went to bed.

That routine continued until gradually, his appetite improved, and he began to feel stronger. He counted the days of "being on the wagon" and proudly exclaimed that he was able to stop drinking on his own.

He and Mom also became more strict with Jennie. They talked to her teachers and made her stay home every weeknight to do homework. She complained, of course, but she did seem to work harder.

On some days, Dad got pretty irritable, and I still tried to stay out of his way. As the weeks passed, though, he seemed to be more predictable. When he wasn't drinking, he didn't have so many **mood swings**, times when he would go from being happy and fun to upset and mean without any apparent reason.

When he was dry, Dad also spent more time with me. Lots of times when he came home from work, we'd go outside and play catch or play basketball together. He liked doing things instead of sitting around, probably because when he sat still he felt like having a drink.

Dad surprised me one morning by saying that he had tickets for us to go to a ball game that night. I was so excited, I could barely wait for school to end. I also worried that he would forget or would not show up. I was used to being disappointed by him, but I prayed that this time it would be different. I hoped that we really would go to the game, just as he had promised. I believed that he had changed because he no longer drank, and I was right!

We had great seats and could see all of the action. We got there early enough to watch the teams warm up, and I even got one player to autograph a game program for me. That was one of the happiest moments of my life.

Dad and I were sharing a bag of popcorn when he left to use the rest room. I didn't mind sitting by myself, because it made me feel older and more responsible.

A weird thing happened though, when he came back to the seats, I smelled beer on his breath. At first, I didn't say anything about it, but when he left again a little while later, I became curious. More than that, I felt worried. I had a sick feeling in my stomach, and my whole body tightened with fear. What if he was drinking again!?

When he returned I asked him, "Did you drink a beer?"

"No, you know I'm on the wagon," he said. "Why do you ask?"

"Well," I hesitated, "your breath smells kind of like beer."

For a while, Dad didn't say anything at all. We watched the game, rooting for our team, but not talking to each other. Finally, he turned to me and said, "Jason, I did have a beer. I swear it was the first time I've had a drink since I quit weeks ago."

"Why?" I asked.

"I smelled beer on his breath."

"I don't know," he replied, "out of habit, I guess. For years, I've drunk beer every time I've ever been to a ball game. It was something I always did, and when I passed the beer line, I couldn't stop myself from having one."

"Are you going to start drinking again?"

"No, I won't," he swore. "I don't know what came over me. I couldn't stop myself from having a beer, but I'm not going to start drinking again. You see, I never really had a drinking problem anyway. I was always able to stop when I wanted to. No, I just felt like having a beer at the game like always, but after tonight, it's back on to the wagon for me."

I believed him and thought he was telling the truth.

"Do me a favor," he said a little while later, "don't tell your mother that I drank that beer, okay. We'll let it be our secret, and no harm will be done."

I nodded, enjoying the game and not wanting to do anything that would ruin it. I didn't pay much attention to what he was saying to me. I don't know if that was the only beer he drank that night or if that was the only time he drank while he was supposed to be "dry." I only cared that my team was winning, and that I was with my Dad, who seemed to like being with me.

Yet, deep inside of me was a voice I didn't want to hear: "What if Dad gets drunk again? If he starts drinking again, he'll lose his job. We'll lose our house! What if he goes for another beer and forgets me? How will I get home?" I tried to put the words out of my head, because they terrified me.

"I saw him in the garage drinking from a bottle of vodka he had kept hidden in his tool box."

CHAPTER 6

Telling Someone

I blamed myself when Dad started drinking a lot again. I thought if we had not gone to the ball game, if he had not been tempted to drink beer that night, if, if, if. . . I didn't know any better. I just felt bad again and told myself that I caused the problems. I didn't realize that his drinking had nothing to do with me.

For a few days, Dad continued to hide his drinking from Mom. He didn't drink a lot, but I caught him sneaking once and Jennie told me that she did, too. Mom was away shopping for groceries when I saw him in the garage drinking from a bottle of vodka he had kept hidden in his tool box.

"What are you looking at?" he angrily said.

"Nothing," I quietly answered.

"That's right," he said. "You saw nothing, and keep it that way. There's nothing wrong with taking a little drink now and then, but if your mother finds out she'll get upset. I don't want you upsetting her, so don't tell her about this. Understand?"

I nodded my head and quickly left.

Eventually, Mom found out that Dad was drinking again, but since he was drinking so much less, she believed him when he said he had it "under control." As long as he kept his drinking to nights and weekends, she was willing to believe him. Otherwise, it meant admitting that the problem was serious again.

Very few alcoholics can simply stop drinking. Their bodies have grown so used to alcohol that they depend on it to keep feeling "normal." Then, when not having a drink, they often think about how and when they can get one, which is called **craving**. The cravings are caused by a physical dependence on alcohol.

Most experts believe that if an alcoholic who has stopped drinking has even one drink, he or she will return to uncontrollable drinking. The illness of alcoholism is an **addiction** to alcohol, which means that it is a habit and that alcoholics who drink cannot stop themselves.

Over the next few weeks, Dad's drinking got even worse than it had been before he was "on the wagon." He stopped helping out around the house, he began coming home late again, he started missing work like he had before, and he got madder than ever.

He thought he should have been able to quit drinking by himself. When he couldn't, he felt like a failure. Then, he drank even more so he wouldn't feel so bad about himself.

The more Dad drank, the more frightened I got, and I think Mom and Jennie felt the same way, too. It was only a matter of time before he would lose his job, crash the car, badly hurt one of us, or die. I was terrified to think about what might happen to us, but I couldn't stop myself.

I guess my fears made me act even quieter than usual, because one day, my teacher, Mr. Ross, talked to me after class.

"Is something bothering you, Jason?" Mr. Ross asked.

"No, I'm okay," I lied. I couldn't say any more. I had been too tired all week to even concentrate at school.

"You seem to be worried a lot lately," he said. "Are you having some problems at home?"

I just looked at him without answering. I was afraid to tell him about Dad's drinking or anger. If I told our family secret, I might really get in bad trouble. If I did tell, then Dad might get in trouble, and I thought that could cause us to lose our house.

Mr. Ross asked me about home again, and I still didn't answer. He told me that I could talk to him anytime, and then he let me leave. I guess he figured that my silence meant there was some kind of problem though, because the next day I had to go talk to Mrs. Paytee, our school counselor.

I was afraid to go to the counselor's office. I didn't understand why I had to go, and I worried that I was in some kind of trouble. What would Dad do to me when he found out? Before I went in I felt like I was in a doctor's office waiting for a shot.

Mrs. Paytee actually had a neat office with lots of posters on the walls. She was about Mom's age and seemed very friendly. She asked me all kinds of questions about myself, and she seemed really interested in my answers. At first, the questions were about what kinds of things I liked to do, my favorite music and TV shows, which subjects I liked in school. She asked me which students were my friends, and she seemed to know a lot of the kids in my class.

"Mrs. Paytee actually had a neat office with lots of posters on the walls."

When she asked about my parents, I didn't say much. I was too embarrassed to say that Dad was drunk every night. It was humiliating to tell anyone, but she was so nice, I found myself telling her things I never told anyone before.

"Is it hard for you to talk about your parents, Jason?" Mrs. Paytee kindly asked.

"I don't know."

"Do you get to spend much time with your Dad?"

"Sometimes."

"What do you like to do together?" she asked.

I didn't know what to answer. I didn't like doing anything with him. Even going to the ball game was bad. I had to say something though, otherwise she might find out the truth. I tried to answer, but no words came to my mouth.

She suggested a few activities, "Does he help you with your homework or take you to the park?"

"He usually doesn't have enough time," I replied, wishing she would stop asking me about him."

Instead, she asked more. Mrs. Paytee knew more about my home life than I expected. I later found out that she thought I came from an alcoholic family, and she was just trying to get me to talk about it.

"Jason, I know that it's hard for some kids to tell outsiders about their homes, especially when they think they shouldn't. You don't have to tell me anything, but I might be able to help you."

I just listened, wondering what to say.

"Are you worried about something at home?"

"Yes, I guess."

"Would you please tell me a little about it?"

She seemed really interested in me and I began to trust her. Before long, I was willing to tell her my family's big secret.

She looked right in my eyes when I talked, and seemed to know how I was feeling about things before I even told her. She understood about alcoholism and how children of alcoholics feel.

Mrs. Paytee asked me if I blamed myself for Dad's drinking, and she explained that it wasn't my fault. She knew I thought he was mad at me, but helped me see that he was really mad at himself.

She told me that I'd done the right thing by talking to her. The school counselor's job is to help students, and she helped me just by listening. I only spoke to her for about an hour, but afterwards, I felt a million times better. It felt great to stop hiding and to say out loud the feelings I'd been having. Telling her the truth about my family was like knowing all the answers on a hard test.

I suppose it would have been good for me to tell someone about Dad's problems sooner. I was too afraid to talk to anyone, but there were a lot of people I could have told. Mom always made excuses for Dad, but maybe I should have told her how I was feeling. I could have talked to one of my grandparents, my Aunt Terry, or another close relative. Mr. Ross would have listened to me. We have neighbors I've known my whole life, and I bet they would have been good to tell. I could have written a letter to one of those newspaper writers who help people with their problems.

I'm thankful that Mrs. Paytee was there to help me. She didn't solve anything really, but she made me feel more secure. Even though Dad continued to drink, I stopped feeling so guilty, like it was my fault all the time. Mainly, I no longer felt so alone. I knew I could always talk more to Mrs. Paytee and sometimes I did.

She promised to speak to my parents, but she also said that she would not be able to stop my father from drinking. Only he could do that.

During the next few weeks, Mrs. Paytee and my parents did have a meeting, but no one told me much about it. Whether or not the meeting with Mrs. Paytee mattered to them, I do know that my visits with her helped me plenty!

CHAPTER 7

From Bad to Worse

Soon after, Dad was sick every morning, and he needed a drink to get strong enough just to go to work. I don't know why Mr. Hardy didn't fire him. Maybe he had! Dad was rarely home at night, and there were some mornings when I found him on the couch sleeping in his clothes.

He practically never talked to me anymore, and when he did it was to yell about noise. Even when I tried to be real quiet, he complained. I thought he just couldn't stand to have me around.

He acted even meaner towards Jennie. She hated him, and I bet she would have run away from home if things had not changed.

There was no way for anyone to tell when Dad's drinking got totally out of control or when it really started hurting his body. His cells were so used to the drug effect of it, he would be in pain if he <u>didn't</u> drink.

Alcohol damages the **cells**. Those are the smallest living parts of the body. There are brain cells, heart cells, and more. An alcoholic's cells in the central nervous system are changed so they can drink more. It becomes "normal" for their cells to have alcohol. After an alcoholic drinks for a long time, some of the cells stop working, which can cause many illnesses and even death.

Alcoholism is called a **progressive illness**, which means that it gradually gets worse and worse. In the early stages, the alcoholic enjoys drinking but may only drink once in a while, like on weekends. Later, the drinker physically **craves** alcohol. When not having a drink, they often think about how and when they can get one. During the late stages of alcoholism, alcoholics <u>must</u> have alcohol to feel better. They will lie, cheat, and give up all responsibilities to get a drink. Alcohol becomes more important than their jobs, homes, families, or self-respect.

This "loss of control" causes them to feel awful about themselves. They think they should be able to stop themselves from drinking, but cannot. When they disappoint the people around them, they feel guilty—like failures. The only way they get any relief is from alcohol.

The life of an alcoholic is like a circle. They're unhappy about drinking so much, but they can't stop themselves. So they drink, feel better for a little while, and then feel bad about themselves because they drank. Then they try to stop for a while but can't. It just goes on and on. They keep drinking and feeling bad. See what I mean?

This circle continues for years, with the alcoholic getting worse and worse and the people around them suffering more and more.

Mom wanted to stop Dad from drinking, but if he did not decide to stop, she had to learn to survive without him. Several things happened within a couple of weeks which showed me that Mom was taking matters into her own hands. She wanted to break the circle. For years, Dad had put her down and took away her confidence. The meeting with Mrs. Paytee must have helped.

Mom threw away Dad's "secret" liquor bottles which he had all over the house: under the bathroom sink, beneath their bed, behind some books on a shelf in the living room, in the back of the hall closet, in a hard to reach kitchen cabinet, and who knows where else!

Maybe throwing out his bottles was not the best thing she could have done. That wouldn't stop him from drinking, but she felt she had to do something.

When Dad discovered them missing, he was furious. He tore open cabinets, threw books all over the room, lifted his bed completely off the frame, and yelled like a crazy man.

I was scared to death watching him. He was so mad that I feared he might kill us all.

*"He tore open cabinets,
threw books all over the room. . ."*

Mom took me and Jennie away. We went out for dinner, but none of us felt hungry. I was angry and afraid. I didn't like seeing Dad act so nuts, and I was mad that Mom didn't say anything about it at the restaurant. No one even mentioned what happened!

When we came back, Dad was gone, which was a relief. The next morning, he was asleep in his car. After that, he would not speak to Mom about anything.

A few days later, Dad called from jail. He had been arrested for **driving under the influence (DUI)** of alcohol. Later, they explained that the police stopped him because his car kept weaving between lanes.

They said his eyes were red and bloodshot and he smelled like beer, so they asked him to take a **sobriety test** to see if he was drunk. He had to put his feet together, stand up straight, put his head back, and close his eyes. He started tipping back and forth like a tall tree in the wind. Next, he had to stand on one foot while counting backwards from 70. The alcohol made him forget which number came before 63!

After he was arrested and taken to the police station, Dad took another test to measure how much alcohol was in his blood. He blew into a machine that gave a reading of his **blood alcohol level (BAL)**. Someone with a measurement of .10 or higher is considered "legally impaired," which means that according to the law, they cannot drive safely and are not allowed to drive. Dad's BAL was much higher than that, so he was charged with **driving while intoxicated (DWI)**. Dad said he only had two beers, but the tests proved that he had had more. One policeman said he was so drunk that he might not have remembered further back than his last two beers!

Mom had to pay money to get Dad out of jail that night. Dad's lawyer told him he would have to go to court in a few weeks, and if the court found him guilty of DWI, he could lose his driver's license, have to pay a large penalty, or might go to jail. Driving while intoxicated is a serious crime.

Finally, Mom looked for help. Dad's drinking was hurting her too much. I think a lot of women would have gotten a divorce if their husbands acted like Dad, but Mom wanted to keep our family together.

Mom's sister, Aunt Terry, spent a day and night at our house, and they talked the whole time. Aunt Terry is a nurse and knows about alcoholism. She made some suggestions to Mom that made a lot of sense.

She convinced Mom to call a **psychologist**, a professional trained to help people understand their feelings. She explained our family's troubles to Dr. Bowers, a psychologist who had worked with many families of alcoholism. She went to him for **therapy**, which means he used his special knowledge and skills to help Mom learn about her thoughts and emotions.

Dr. Bowers helped her to see that she could not make Dad stop drinking, but that it was important for her to take care of herself. Even if he stayed the same, she could change how she acted and felt. She learned to stop making excuses, and to see herself as worthwhile and separate from him.

Dad knew that Mom went to Dr. Bowers twice a week for therapy, but he refused to go with her. He said that there was nothing wrong with him. He admitted that he drank a lot, but he said that it wasn't a problem for him. So, Mom went to Dr. Bowers without him, and she learned about alcoholism, codependency, and what she could do to make her own life better.

Dr. Bowers showed Mom she had options:

* She could continue living with Dad the way things were, and he would probably get worse. He might get sick and have to go to the hospital. He might die from an alcohol-caused disease or in a car accident while driving drunk. He would not get any nicer to us, and chances were that he would become meaner, possibly badly hurting us.

* She could ask Dad to move out of the house, and then either get a divorce or stay separated unless he changed.

* Mom, Jennie, and I could move out of the house. We could stay with a relative or go to a **shelter**, a special place for families to live when it is unsafe to stay in their homes.

* Mom decided to try **guided intervention**. That is a planned action when people get together to convince an alcoholic to quit drinking.

Given the choice of staying with Dad as a drunk, breaking up the family, or trying intervention, Mom felt that our greatest chance at happiness would be if Dad quit drinking. If he refused to get professional help, then Mom said she would ask him to move out.

CHAPTER 8

Intervention

Eight of us sat in Mr. Hardy's office waiting for Dad. We were the intervention "team." Like any other kind of team, we had to work together to win. In this case, "winning" meant convincing Dad that he had to quit drinking. Dr. Bowers was like our team captain. He had talked to each of us to explain what we were supposed to do during the intervention meeting with Dad.

The plan was that we would all meet in Mr. Hardy's office. Since he was Dad's boss, that would be a sure way to get Dad to come without being suspicious. Dr. Bowers said that if Dad knew we were going to be there to confront him, he probably would not show up.

We were all supposed to write a list of things to say to him. We could say anything we wanted to, but it was most important to tell him how we felt about his drinking. That was actually the first time any of our family said anything about our feelings to each other. I told Mrs. Paytee my feelings, and Mom had talked to her sister and Dr. Bowers, but none of us had ever talked to each other!

Intervention meetings can be painful times, and Mom wasn't sure whether or not I should be included. She thought it might be too scary for me, but I wanted to be there. I wanted to tell him my feelings. I asked Mrs. Paytee about it, and she also thought it would be okay for me to attend.

Besides Mom, Jennifer, Dr. Bowers, Mr. Hardy, and me, the other team members were Aunt Terry, who was there to support Mom, Dad's friend, Jack, and a surprise visitor from out of town, Grandma, Dad's mother. She was chosen for the team because she loved Dad and wanted him to be healthy, and also because Dr. Bowers said that Dad would probably act better with her there.

We had a plan for the intervention, just like a sports team makes a game plan. To get Dad to come, Mr. Hardy's secretary would tell him that he was wanted in the boss's office. After he was told why we were there, each of us would take turns talking. If he left the room, Jack and Mr. Hardy were assigned the job of trying to get him to come back inside. If Dad agreed to quit drinking, Dr. Bowers would arrange for him to go to an alcohol **treatment center**, which is a special type of hospital where alcoholics go to stop drinking. Mom had packed a suitcase for him, just in case he agreed to go.

Having an intervention session with an alcoholic is not always possible or successful. It takes a lot of planning. For it to work, there have to be loved ones who are willing to be honest with the alcoholic. There has to be a trained professional leading the group. The alcoholic must stay to listen to the intervention members. Solutions for the problem, such as having a treatment center available, have to be suggested. Finally, the alcoholic has to agree to try quitting and get professional help immediately. If he or she agrees to go in a few days, it may be too late. All of these things have to happen for the intervention to be successful.

"What's this all about?" Dad muttered, looking at all of us from the doorway.

"Please come in and sit down, Tom," Mr. Hardy said from a seat behind his large desk.

Dad didn't move. He looked around the room. "Jack? Mother? What are you doing here?"

Grandma went to him and kissed his cheek. We were all supposed to stay in our seats, and I wondered what would happen when she broke the rule. "Tom, honey," she said, sounding a lot like my Mom when she talks to me, "We all love you and want you to listen to what we have to say. Come sit next to me." She took his hand and they sat down. I bet if Mom or Jennie had tried that, Dad would have pushed them away. Grandma knew what she was doing!

*"We all love you and want you to listen
to what we have to say."*

"Would someone explain to me what's going on here," Dad asked. His voice sounded shaky, like he was scared.

"I'm Dr. Bowers, Tom. You know everyone else in the room. Susan asked me to come here today with the others to talk to you about your drinking."

"There's nothing wrong with me. I can handle my drinking!" Dad shouted.

"We'd like you to listen to what everyone says," Dr. Bowers continued. "If you still don't think you have a problem, fine; but it's important to the people in this room to have the chance to say what they came here to tell you. The only thing I'm asking of you is that you listen to each of them. Will you do that, please?"

"I don't know," Dad said. "I don't think I want to."

"Will you do it for me, Tom?" Mom asked.

"Who's idea was this anyway?"

"I came a long way," Grandma said. "We only want you to listen.

"I don't like this."

"What are you afraid of?" Jack asked.

"I'm not afraid of anything," Dad said, moving around uncomfortably in his chair. "I just think this is a stupid idea. I don't like it. I'm not staying."

"You want to leave, Tom?" Dr. Bowers questioned.

"Yeah, I sure do."

"I know exactly what you're thinking," he continued. "You want to walk out of here and get a drink."

"No I don't," Dad replied.

"You're lying, Tom," Dr. Bowers said. "You've been lying about your drinking for a long time. It's not your fault, but you can do something about it. It's up to you. You can either leave now and get drunk again, or you can stay because everyone in this room cares about you and wants the chance to say something. What are you going to do?"

Dad didn't answer for almost a minute. Finally, he nodded his head and quietly answered, "Okay, I'll stay."

Jack talked first. He and Dad had been friends since high school. He was funny and even had all of us laughing at a couple of stories about their early days of drinking together. He mainly spoke about good times, but he also mentioned that Dad's drinking got in the way of their friendship.

Mr. Hardy went next. He complimented Dad on being a good worker when he was sober. "Tom, you were one of the finest employees I ever had before alcohol got in the way. Our company's insurance program will pay for professional treatment to help you quit drinking, and I promise you will still have your job waiting for you." He ended by saying that Dad could not work for him anymore if he did not go to the treatment center that day.

Aunt Terry only spoke for a couple of minutes. She sat next to Mom, who cried off and on throughout the meeting. Aunt Terry told Dad that she liked him when he and Mom got married. She asked him to stop drinking because it was hurting her to see Mom and the rest of our family so unhappy.

Dad did not like what he heard. The rule was that he could not interrupt anyone while they talked, but he could reply to each one when they had finished. He seemed too embarrassed to look at the people while they spoke, and when it was his turn to answer, he usually only sighed or said something like, "I can't believe this is happening," or "I don't need to listen to this."

My Turn to Talk

After Grandma read through her list, she told him about how one of her brothers died from alcoholism and that she prayed her son would quit. Then, it was my turn to talk.

My heart beat faster than if I had run a race. Sweat covered my forehead but my fingers were as cold as popsicles. I didn't know if I could get the words out of my mouth, but I wanted to. I knew that this intervention was important to saving our family. I tried to be brave, to help my Dad. In the beginning, I was nervous, and I think I sounded kind of stupid. Even before my turn, I was worried just thinking about what I was going to say.

"You know when you stopped drinking that time a few months ago? You spent time with me. Remember?"

Dad looked at me and said, "Yes."

"You were like a regular Dad, then. You were really different. I thought maybe everything would be okay until you started drinking again.

"Now, I'm afraid again. I'm afraid you'll hit me, or you might kill us when you drive. Everyone always says how dangerous it is to drink and drive, and you do it all the time. When I drive in the car with you, I'm always scared.

"I still remember the time you started a fire in the kitchen, because you forgot to turn off the stove. Almost every night while I'm lying in bed, I get afraid that it will happen again, that I'll die in my sleep.

"Mom tells me that everything is okay, but I know it's not. I heard her tell Aunt Terry that we don't have *any* money left. What will we eat?

"Most of my pants are too tight. Every time I ask Mom when I can get some new pants, she says she'll take care of it in a few days.

"Everyone says that the reason we're having so many problems is because you drink so much alcohol. They told me that you can't stop yourself unless you get someone to help you. I'll help Dad, really."

Dad's face was in his hands, but he looked up at me. His eyes were red and he looked like he was going to cry. He shook his head and sighed, "There's nothing you can do to help, Jason. You can't help."

"Maybe I can get a job after school," I said. "I can hang out with you at home so you won't drink."

Then I realized what I had said, and I began to cry. "I'm sorry about what happened at the ball game, Dad. If it wasn't for me, you wouldn't have started drinking again. It's all my fault." I cried so hard, I couldn't talk anymore.

Dad got up from his chair and kneeled in front of me. He hugged me and said, "It's not your fault, Jason. Believe me, I don't want to hurt you."

I hugged him hard, wishing that I could squeeze the alcoholism out of his body. "Please make it okay again, Dad," I quietly said into his ear. "Please go to that place where Dr. Bowers said they will help you. Please stop drinking."

I felt really embarrassed because I was crying in front of everyone. I felt embarrassed for Dad too, because he was crying with me.

Jennie's List

When it was Jennifer's turn to talk, she did not cry at all. She was <u>angry</u>.

"Dr. Bowers told me to make a list of things to say to you, Dad. So here goes:

"I wish you would go away and never come back. You're always yelling at me and telling me what to do, but I think you're really sick. "

"You yell at me for the way I dress or how I wear my hair, but you should see yourself. Sometimes I see you sleeping on the couch with your clothes on. You always need a shave, your hair is messy, you look like one of those bums that live on downtown park benches. Plus you smell bad! It's not fair for you to yell at me for how I look when you don't care about yourself.

"You get mad at me for doing badly in school, but I think you're the one who has the problems. I get grounded or hit for getting drunk or skipping school, but what about you? You're always drunk! I know you go out and get drunk and sometimes don't even go to work. So you're worse than me. I wish your boss would punch you in the face sometime so you could see what it feels like to get hit."

Dad would not stay in his seat for this, and when Dr. Bowers told him to sit down, he told Dr. Bowers, "Shut up. She's my daughter, and I'm not going to take this from her. She better show some respect or I'll slap her right here in front of all of you. I don't care, she has no right to talk to me this way. I'm her father!"

"Sit down!" Dr. Bowers loudly said. "Give her the chance to say what she wants to say, and then you can talk."

"You're not telling me what I can and can't do, buddy," he said to Dr. Bowers. "In fact, I'm through. I've taken as much as I'm going to take. Forget you all!"

Then, Dad ran out the door.

Mr. Hardy and Jack quickly walked out of the room to get him to come back. They were doing exactly what Dr. Bowers said they should do if Dad left.

Grandma talked to Jennifer, trying to calm her down. Mom was really upset, and Aunt Terry held her hand. I looked at them and didn't know what to do. Then I looked at Dr. Bowers, who smiled and quietly said to me, "I think this is going to work out just fine." Then he winked!

Sure enough, Dad came back into the room with the other men, and they all sat down. He angrily stared at Jennie.

She continued in her sassiest voice "Let's see," checking her list, "you look ugly, you smell bad, you skip work to get drunk, you never listen. Right, you never listen. You always think you know everything. Even when I've done nothing wrong, you call me a liar. It doesn't matter what I say, because you don't care.

"You think I'm supposed to be some kind of maid or servant or something. Whenever you see a dirty dish or anything at all messy, you always blame me. What about the time you found an empty beer can on the bathroom floor. You accused me of drinking and leaving it there. You said I'm not allowed to ever drink, and you called me a filthy slob. How do you think that made me feel? It wasn't even mine. You were the one who left it there but were too drunk to remember. You pushed me into the wall in the bathroom and started swearing at me. Then, you pulled my hair so my head was at my knees, yelling at me to clean it up. I wished you were dead, and I wished I had a gun so I could have killed you."

Dad just sat there with his head turned away from her. He didn't say anything.

Dr. Bowers spoke to Jennie, "You have good reasons to be angry with your father, don't you?"

"I sure do," she said.

"I also asked you to talk to him about quitting. What else would you like to say?"

"I guess I hope you go to that treatment center or whatever. It's hard for me to believe you'll ever quit drinking, because I think you love getting drunk more than anything. So, if you don't quit, I hope you never come back to live with us. That's all I have to say."

"Is there anything you would like to tell Jennifer, Tom?" Dr. Bowers asked.

"No," he said, sounding mad and hurt.

"That's fine."

"Jennifer, perhaps someday you will forgive your father for the way he has treated you.

"Tom, you have deeply hurt your daughter. She may resent you for a long time. Only through **sobriety**, by no longer drinking, will you have any possibility of winning back her love.

"In treatment, you can both have the opportunity to honestly talk and listen to each other. There are no magic answers for either of you. If you work at it, you may be able to discover love for each other once again."

Dad's Decision

Mom talked longer than anyone, and several times she was interrupted by her tears. She complained about the money problems, his lack of responsibility, that he sometimes disappeared, and that he did not take part in our home life. She cried when she told him that she did not think he could love her anymore and that he never wanted to hold her or kiss her. She said that she would want him to move out of the house if he did not go to the treatment center. Mom promised to help him quit drinking, but that if he refused, she would want a divorce.

Dr. Bowers thanked Dad for staying to hear us, and he thanked us for caring enough to be there for Dad. Instead of asking Dad to respond to everyone or even speak up for himself, Dr. Bowers explained what would happen to him if he agreed to go to the treatment center.

Like most alcoholics, Dad was in **denial**. He was too ashamed to admit that his drinking was out of control. He said he could handle drinking, and that he would cut back on his own, but Dr. Bowers said that would not work. He reminded Dad that his friendships, job, health, and family, all depended upon his going to the treatment center. Still, Dad said he did not want to go.

He promised to shape up at work, but Mr. Hardy said that was not good enough. He tried to convince us that he really would give up drinking, but we did not believe him. He asked Mom if she would give him another chance, but she said, "No."

Finally, he agreed. He said he did not think he needed to, but that he would go to please everyone. So, the intervention worked. We *won!*

After taking care of a few details and saying good-bye to everyone, Dad was driven by Jack across town to the treatment center.

CHAPTER 9

Treatment

I hoped Dad's alcoholism cure would be quick, that he'd be home soon, and our problems at home would suddenly disappear. Instead, Dad had to stay at the treatment center for over one month.

I worried about him. For the first two weeks we were not allowed to visit him or even talk to him on the phone. It seemed like he was in prison, and I even wondered if that was where he really was. Sometimes, I imagined that he had died.

Finally, one Sunday, we were allowed to see him. I visited with Mom, but Jennie didn't want to go along.

The treatment center was in a smaller building next to the hospital where I was born. It had brightly painted walls, long halls, a couple of meeting rooms the size of my classroom, a cafeteria that wasn't even as big as the one at school, and a lot of small bedrooms, one of which Dad shared with another man. It wasn't a very fancy place, like a hotel, but it was much more homey than a hospital.

We met Dad in a recreation room that had a television, some couches, and shelves with books and magazines. I thought he might have to wear one of those hospital gowns that doesn't close all the way in the back, but he wore regular clothes.

Dad was nervous about seeing us. He acted kind of embarrassed about being locked up there. I think he felt like a failure, because he had been unable to control his drinking. He still did not completely accept that he really needed to be there. He was pretty quiet, and I felt sorry for him.

Dad told us that when he had first arrived, he mainly rested. He had a complete medical examination to see how much his years of heavy drinking had affected his body. Every day during his **detoxification**— while alcohol leaves the body— the nurses checked his temperature and blood pressure. He was given medicine to help him sleep, and liquids, vitamins, and minerals to help his body get healthy.

With proper nutrition in his diet, he began to get physically stronger. He learned what his body needed to stay healthy, so he could continue to eat well when he returned home.

If alcoholics do not satisfy the cravings by drinking, they start having **withdrawal symptoms**— their body reacts badly to not getting alcohol. They might become shaky, have headaches, get hot and cold spells, feel dizzy and sick to their stomachs, and act confused or depressed. In the worst cases, they might have the **D.T.'s (delirium tremens)**, which are terrible experiences like having nightmares while being awake. An alcoholic feels sicker from *not* drinking than from drinking!

It took a few days before Dad started to think clearly. He didn't want to be there at all, and said he had only gone because of the pressure from everyone at the intervention meeting. During withdrawal, he had trouble sleeping, his hands kept shaking, and he was depressed a lot of the time. Gradually, as the alcohol no longer filled his cells, he started feeling better. Then, he began to understand that he really did need to be there.

He showed us his room. It only had two beds, a dresser he shared with his roommate, and two small desks. On his was a picture of the four of us that was taken one Christmas. Mom complimented him on how tidy the room was, and Dad said that it was a rule for him to make his bed and clean up every day. Mom joked that he could take care of the housework when he came home.

There were several rules in the treatment center. Patients had to go to all meals, were assigned daily tasks (like washing dishes or sweeping the halls), and had to do homework. They also had to exercise. They were not allowed to leave the center or make telephone calls, except if there was an emergency.

They were required to attend lectures and films that explained how alcohol affects the body and how a healthy diet helps prevent someone from wanting to drink alcohol.

"Mom complimented him on how tidy the room was."

He also had therapy sessions, both alone with a psychologist and with groups of other patients.

Every day, he had to attend an **Alcoholics Anonymous (AA)** meeting at the treatment center. Those were groups of alcoholics who talked about their experiences and got support from each other for not drinking. At the meetings, the individuals only used their first names and many introduced themselves in the way that Dad did, "Hello, my name is Tom, and I am an alcoholic."

At the AA meetings, there were alcoholics who had just stopped drinking and others who had quit for many years. Those meetings showed Dad that other people had the same problems that he did, and that they could get better. People in the treatment program that Dad entered were required to attend meetings for at least two years, even after they went back to living at home.

Alcoholics Anonymous is the largest organization in the world for people who need help to stop drinking. AA groups are in cities and towns all over North America and in many other countries throughout the world. There are also other kinds of support groups for alcoholics besides AA, but it is the most well-known.

Our visit only lasted for an hour, and then we had to go home. While we drove, Mom asked me how I felt.

"Okay, I guess," I said. "It was strange to see Dad acting so sad."

"Why do you think he's sad?" she asked.

"I don't know. Maybe he misses being home or they're mean to him there. Maybe he's sad because he can't drink beer there."

"Do you miss him?"

"Kind of," I answered. I wasn't ready to tell Mom how I really felt—that it was more relaxing with him gone.

"He'll be home pretty soon," she said. "Then everything will be good."

I listened, but I did not really believe her. I was too used to being lonely, afraid, and hurt inside. I hoped that she was right, but it would take a long time before I was convinced.

While Dad was away at the treatment center, Mom continued to see Dr. Bowers for therapy sessions. She needed to understand how Dad's alcoholism affected our whole family, and she had to think about how life would be different without Dad drinking. He suggested that she go to **Alanon** meetings, groups like AA for loved-ones of alcoholics, where she could get support from others whose families had similar problems.

During that time, life around the house began to improve. The therapy helped Mom to change. She stopped trying to control everything, and she let Jennie and me make more of our own decisions. Mom also sat down with me more and tried to help me to express my feelings. I guess you could say I started to feel more loved and cared for.

Jennifer also had therapy sessions with Dr. Bowers. He wanted her to talk about her anger, and to see that Dad's drinking was an important reason for her troubles. Dr. Bowers wanted Jennie to try improving her relationship with Dad even before he came home.

To further help her see that alcoholism is a family problem, she went to **Alateen** meetings, which are groups for teenagers to share their experiences of living in homes with alcoholism. At the Alateen meetings, Jennie was able to see that her anger at Dad was normal, and that a lot of kids felt the same way about their parents. By talking about it, she began to feel less angry, and started to realize that Dad behaved so badly towards her because of alcoholism.

At first, Jennie didn't want to go to the meetings, but after the first couple, she looked forward to them. She even made some new friends there. They had a special friendship, because they had such similar experiences with parents who were alcoholics. Eventually, she was ready to see Dad again.

"She even made some new friends there."

We also attended **family therapy** sessions, with Dr. Bowers and Dad at the center. In those meetings, we got the chance to talk about our feelings and also to plan for Dad's return. Even after he came home, we continued going to family therapy because getting Dad to stop drinking was only the first step. He had to continue to not drink, and we had to learn how to live together without him drinking. It sounds easy, but it meant a new way of life for us.

We made a contract, an agreement, with each other that there would be no alcohol in our house. That wasn't a problem for me, of course, but it meant that not only Dad, but Mom, Jennie, and visitors would not be allowed to drink in our house. Some alcoholic families choose to let others, besides the alcoholic, drink at home, but we did not.

Once he was out of the treatment center, Dad agreed that he would not go to bars, and he would not drink anywhere— not at business lunches, fancy restaurants, barbeques, ball games: not anywhere!

He would be tempted to begin drinking at home. Just like going to the ball game made him think about having beer, he was used to drinking at home. Only, this time he had to resist! So we made up ideas of things he could do to stop himself when he had cravings.

Jennie promised that she would not drink until she was legally old enough, if ever. She said that if friends drank at parties, she would refuse even though that might make her seem "uncool." She also agreed not to ride in cars if the driver had been drinking. To drive with a drinker would not only be stupid, but it could also be deadly!

Another thing we talked about in the family therapy sessions was how we would relate to one another when Dad got home. He had to stop being angry and respect the rest of us.

Drinking and being drunk used to take up most of his time. Without alcohol he would have much more time on his hands. In the therapy meetings, we made plans for how he would better spend that time. A lot of the plans included being with me, Mom, and Jennie, and I really hoped that those plans would work.

CHAPTER 10

Coming Home

The treatment center helped Dad in many ways. Most importantly, he ended his drinking habit. He had been drunk practically every day for several years— except that short period when he tried to quit— so not drinking for even a week was difficult for him.

While in treatment, Dad quit denying his problem and finally admitted that he had not been able to control his drinking. He learned how alcohol affected his body and mind, and that it was not his fault that he drank so much. He had a disease: alcoholism. He accepted this fact and also that he did need to quit.

Not everyone who enters a treatment center or even gets sober is able to stay away from booze. Many alcoholics return to drinking, and their problems often get even worse. That's what happened before when Dad tried to quit. The meetings and therapy sessions showed him that support from other people would really help him stay sober.

He learned not to be embarrassed about being an alcoholic. He heard stories from people at Alcoholics Anonymous meetings which helped him see that it was for his own good to let others know that he could not drink.

Learning about alcoholism and recovery convinced Dad that staying sober was the most important thing in his life. Otherwise, he would lose his family, job, friends, and health. He could have no chance for lasting love or happiness. He made a commitment to not drink anymore.

Our family therapy sessions prepared us for his return, but talking about it and actually having him back were two different things.

I was afraid that when Dad came home everything would be the same again. I expected to catch him secretly drinking in the garage, to find him fully dressed and asleep on the couch, and to have him angry again. I wanted a happy home, but I didn't believe we'd have one. How could I?

The day he came home, we acted like nothing had ever been wrong. Mom cooked a special meal, but Dad was not too hungry, so she blamed herself for cooking the wrong food. Jennie pretty much ignored him, and she went out with friends after dinner instead of sticking around too long. I stayed quiet and out of the way reading a book. It was like having a stranger in the house; no one was sure what to say to him.

In those first days back home, Dad was sober, but that did not mean he was always happy or nice. Sometimes, he seemed moody. He even yelled at us and blamed others just as he had when he was drinking.

Mr. Hardy kept his job for him as promised, but Dad worried more about work. He felt he had to prove himself after doing so poorly because of drinking. He also thought his clients might not like him if he wasn't drinking.

As the months passed though, Dad began changing. He was discovering who he was without alcohol. His mind was clearer and he began to feel good about himself in new ways:

* He did not think about <u>never</u> drinking again, but as he put it, "Jason, I'm taking one day at a time." At the end of the day, he could look back and feel proud that he had not gotten drunk that day. Gradually, the days added up to weeks and then months.

* Dad continued going to Alcoholics Anonymous meetings every week. When he felt especially unsure of himself, he went to meetings every night! Sometimes, I wished he would stay home, but he'd say, "I go to the A.A. meetings because I love you, not because I want to be away. The meetings help me to love myself and you, too."

* He started new routines. Instead of walking in the house after work and having a beer, he took a long walk when he came home.

He either went alone or one of us went with him. I loved those long walks together, because we talked about all kinds of things, and Dad seemed interested in me.

* We started having family meetings on Sunday nights when we all had a chance to say our feelings. This was a brand new activity for us, because during those years of Dad's drinking, we never talked about our feelings! We also made plans and shared ideas about how we thought our family life could be better. Mom usually had thoughts about how everyone could help clean up around the house more!

* Dad tried to be home on time for dinner every night, and we ate family meals together. Not only did that keep him away from bars and old habits, but it also showed us that he cared about the family.

* Dad started laughing more. We all began to enjoy being together.

I started to change, too. I no longer went to bed afraid, and instead felt loved when Mom or Dad came into my room to say good night.

Dad began to listen to me and to treat me with more respect, so I began to trust myself more. I quit hiding my feelings so much and felt safe enough to be happy or sad. No one feels great all of the time, but it's better to have all kinds of feelings than none at all.

As I became more confident, I also made a few friends. I even invited them to my house and went to theirs. One of the happiest times I can remember is the first time a friend stayed over night. We stayed up real late watching television and playing games. It was really fun, and not once did I worry about secrets or Dad getting drunk or mad. In fact, he took us out for hamburgers!

Jennie had a harder time accepting that Dad really changed. He had been home for about two months and Jennie still resented him. He didn't hit her again, but they still argued a lot. I think she wanted him to fail with his sobriety so that he would eventually have to leave.

One day when a friend of hers was at our house "studying," Mom caught them drinking a bottle of wine. Mom yelled a little and said Jennie's friend had to go home. As Mom and Jennie left to drive her friend home, Jennie put the half-empty bottle on the kitchen counter. She must have known Dad would walk in there, and I bet she did it on purpose to see if she could tempt him to drink it.

Sure enough, Dad did find the bottle there. He didn't know I was watching him from the other room. When Dad saw the bottle, it was like he had seen a ghost! He sat down at the kitchen table and stared at it from a few feet away. He called out, "Susan?" But there was no answer. He hollered louder, "Susan? Jennifer? Is anyone home?"

I don't know why, but I remained silent, watching him to see what he would do. For two or three minutes, he just sat there looking at the bottle.

Then, he got up from his chair and walked over to it. He touched the end with his finger and sniffed the scent of wine. I suppose that was the first time he even smelled alcohol since he went into treatment. He picked up the bottle and gently held it. He looked so familiar with it in his hand.

I didn't know what he was going to do next. I was afraid he would drink the wine, and I surprised myself by running into the kitchen saying, "Dad, what are you doing?"

He was startled and almost dropped the bottle. "Where did this come from," he asked in a low voice.

I didn't answer.

He looked at me staring at him. There he was holding a half-drunk bottle of wine. It was a scene out of the past, a time he wanted to stay in the past. "Hey Jason," he said, "let's pour this wine down the drain together." He put his free arm around my shoulder and emptied the wine in the sink. Then he tossed the bottle in the trash, picked me up in his arms, and said, "I love you."

"Let's pour this wine down the drain together."

When Jennie came home, there was no ugly fight, as I expected. Instead, we sat down and talked about family rules. Jennie broke her promise by drinking wine <u>and</u> bringing alcohol into the house. Dad felt betrayed by her, but he still treated her with respect. It was obvious that she had to face some consequences. We discussed honesty and trust. Everyone had a chance to say what they thought would be a fair punishment, and Jennie's suggestion was the one chosen.

After that, Jennie started to change a little, too. She was still a teenager and testing her limits—that wouldn't change. She saw that

Mom and Dad cared about her, and started to see that she was an important, worthwhile, special person. Slowly, and with time, Jennie forgave Dad for the horrible way he treated her when he was drinking. Then, she was able to love him.

It has been over one year since Dad last took a drink. We had a small party—with a cake instead of booze—to celebrate his first year of sobriety.

When I'm a grown up with kids of my own, I hope that Dad has still gone without another drink. We'll look back at this time as long, long ago—maybe too long ago to even remember what it was like when he drank. I was lucky. My Dad got sober and changed.

Not all alcoholic parents admit that they cannot control their drinking. Their kids face the same kind of terrible behavior that I lived with when my Dad was still drinking. Those kids need to talk to someone who will listen. My school counselor helped me, but a sober parent, good adult friend, or close relative can also help. Unhappiness and guilt will not get better by keeping secrets. It's important to have feelings and to talk about them. Hiding from problems does not make them go away.

Children of alcoholics can find happiness, self-worth, and love. I know, because I have.

"Children of alcoholics can find happiness, self-worth, and love. I know, because I have."

Glossary

addiction — A habit which cannot be easily stopped, such as drinking alcohol.

Alanon — Groups of loved-ones of alcoholics who attend meetings for support and a better understanding about alcoholism and the problems it causes families.

Alateen — Groups of teen-aged children of alcoholics who attend meetings for support and a better understanding about alcoholism and how it affects them.

alcohol — A chemical in beer, wine, and other liquor.

alcoholic — Someone who drinks so much alcohol that they cannot easily stop themselves from drinking.

Alcoholics Anonymous (AA) — An organization of small groups of people who have meetings and support each other to stop drinking.

alcoholism — A progressive disease of alcohol addiction.

blackouts — When someone forgets things they did and said.

blood alcohol level (BAL) — A measurement which shows how much alcohol is contained in someone's blood.

cells — The smallest living parts of the body. There are brain cells, heart cells, and more.

central nervous system — The brain is the main part of this body system, which controls body movements, the senses, thoughts, emotions, and even dreams.

codependent — Someone who has changed their behavior due to another's alcoholism or other addiction.

craves, cravings — When an alcoholic thinks about how and when they can get a drink. Cravings are caused by a physical dependence on alcohol.

D.T.'s (delirium tremens) — Terrible experiences like having nightmares while being awake that some alcoholics have when they first stop drinking.

denial — When someone does not admit to having a problem.

depressant — A drug that lowers the energy of the central nervous system.

detoxification, detox — What happens when an alcoholic first stops drinking, and alcohol leaves the body.

drinking in moderation — Being able to drink a little at a time, like one or two drinks.

driving under the influence (DUI), driving while intoxicated (DWI) — Illegally driving a car, motorcycle, or other motor vehicle while having such a high blood alcohol level that it is unsafe to be driving.

drunk — The feeling of being light headed or dizzy, having slower thinking and actions, and being sick from drinking alcohol.

family therapy — Working on shared problems with a professional therapist with other family members.

guided intervention — A planned action when people get together to convince an alcoholic to quit drinking.

hangovers — Feeling sick after being drunk.

heredity — Being born with certain kinds of characteristics inherited from one or both parents.

mood swings — When someone goes from being happy and fun to upset and mean without any apparent reason.

on the wagon — Not drinking anymore.

progressive illness — A disease that gradually gets worse and worse.

psychologist — A professional trained to help people understand their feelings. (see **therapist)**

recovering alcoholic — An alcoholic who stops drinking.

secrets — In alcoholic families it is often an unspoken rule not to tell other people about the alcoholic's drinking or other family problems.

shelter — A special place for families to live when it is unsafe to stay in their homes.

sober — Not drinking any more.

sobriety test — The way that law enforcement officials determine whether or not someone is drunk or has a high blood alcohol level.

social drinkers — People who can enjoy drinking once in a while without having to keep drinking.

stimulant — A drug that increases energy levels in the central nervous system.

therapist — A professional trained to help people understand their feelings, such as a psychiatrist, psychologist, marriage and family counselor, school counselor, etc.

therapy — Working on improving behavior or feelings through specific actions, typically being guided by a therapist.

treatment center — A special type of hospital where alcoholics go to stop drinking.

withdrawal symptoms — When an alcoholic reacts badly to not getting alcohol. They might become shaky, have headaches, get hot and cold spells, feel dizzy and sick to their stomachs, and act confused or depressed.

About the Authors

Lindsey Hall and Leigh Cohn are the co-authors of numerous books that help people. They often speak to groups on personal growth, are married, and have two children. Lindsey is also a soft sculpture designer and has a B.A. in Psychology from Stanford University. Leigh is a former teacher and has an M.A.T. in English Education from Northwestern University.

Rosemary E. Lingenfelter is a mother, artist, and elementary educator.

FREE:
The Gürze Bookshelf Catalogue
This catalogue features an extensive list of books and tapes from various publishers on children of alcoholics, eating disorders, personal growth, self-esteem, co-dependency, addiction, and more.

Dear Kids of Alcoholics
Young readers (ages 8-17) will identify with Jason, a boy whose father is an alcoholic. Jason explains facts about alcoholism with touching stories about his dad's sensitivity to alcohol, destructive behavior, and recovery process.

Dear Kids of Alcoholics: Guidebook*
This companion booklet includes topics for discussion, questions, exercises, and activities to help young readers get the most out of the book, *Dear Kids of Alcoholics*.

* For teachers, parents, counselors and groups

- -

Order Form:

I am enclosing $_____ for the following (including shipping):
    *** California residents, please add 6.5% sales tax.

____**FREE: The Gürze Bookshelf Catalogue**
____copies of **Dear Kids of Alcoholics** $6.95 ($1.75 shipping)
____copies of **Dear Kids of Alcoholics** 5 or more copies
    $5.50 each ($.75 each shipping)
____copies of **Dear Kids of Alcoholics: Guidebook**
    $4.95 ($1.75 shipping)

NAME _____

ADDRESS _____

CITY/STATE/ZIP _____

PHONE _____

*Send payment to: Gürze Books, Box 2238, Carlsbad CA 92008
or call (619)434-7533*